City Safari

Raccoon

Isabel Thomas

Heinemann
LIBRARY
Chicago, Illinois

© 2014 Heinemann Library
an imprint of Capstone Global Library, LLC
Chicago, Illinois

To contact Capstone Global Library please phone 800-747-4992,
or visit our website www.capstonepub.com

Edited by Dan Nunn, Rebecca Rissman, and Helen Cox
Cannons
Designed by Tim Bond
Original illustrations © Capstone Global Library Ltd 2014
Picture research by Mica Brancic
Production by Helen McCreath
Originated by Capstone Global Library Ltd
Printed and bound in China

17 16 15 14 13
10 9 8 7 6 5 4 3 2 1

Library of Congress Cataloging-in-Publication Data
Thomas, Isabel, 1980- author.
  Raccoon / Isabel Thomas.
    pages cm.—(City safari)
  Includes bibliographical references and index.
  ISBN 978-1-4329-8811-1 (hb)—ISBN 978-1-4329-8818-0 (pb) 1.
Raccoon—Juvenile literature. 2. Raccoon—Behavior—Juvenile
literature. 3. Urban animals—Juvenile literature. I. Title.

QL737.C26T46 2014
599.76′32—dc23   2013017411

Acknowledgments
The author and publisher are grateful to the following for
permission to reproduce copyright material: Alamy p. 10 (©
tbkmedia.de); flickr p.21; FLPA pp. 7 (Minden Pictures/Michael
Durham). 8 (Malcolm Schuyl), 14 (S & D & K Maslowski); Getty
Images p. 9 (© RLO'Leary); Naturepl.com pp. 5 (© Florian
Möllers), 6 (© Rolf Nussbaumer), 13 (© B&S Draker), 19 (© Ingo
Bartussek), 23 nest (© Ingo Bartussek), 23 predator (© B&S
Draker); Photoshot pp. 18 & 23 mat (© Juniors Tierbildarchiv);
Shutterstock pp. 4 (© davewright321), 8 (© Emily Veinglory), 11
(© janr34), 12 (© Becky Sheridan), 16 (© Jay Stuhlmiller), 17 (©
Charles Brutlag), 20, 23 den & 23 kit (all © Gerald A. DeBoer), 23
nocturnal (© eddtoro); SuperStock p. 15 (Flirt).

Front cover photograph of a raccoon reproduced with
permission of Shutterstock (© Nickolay Stanev). Back cover
photograph of a raccoon playing in water reproduced with
permission of Shutterstock (© Becky Sheridan).

We would like to thank Michael Bright for his invaluable help in
the preparation of this book.

Every effort has been made to contact copyright holders of any
material reproduced in this book. Any omissions will be rectified
in subsequent printings if notice is given to the publisher.

Warning!

Never touch wild animals or their homes. Some wild animals carry diseases. Scared animals may bite or scratch you. Raccoons leave dark, tube-shaped droppings. Never touch animal droppings.

Note About Spotter Icon

Your eyes, ears, and nose can tell you if a raccoon is nearby. Look for these clues as you read the book, and find out more on page 22.

Contents

Some words are shown in bold, **like this**.
You can find them in the glossary on page 23.

Who Has Been Caught Stealing from a Dumpster?

Shiny eyes. A furry mask. A bushy, ringed tail. It's a raccoon!

Cities and towns are not just home to people.

Cities and towns are home to wild animals, too.

Come on a city safari. Find out if raccoons are living near you.

Why Do Raccoons Live in Towns and Cities?

Most raccoons live in the country.

They find shelter, food, and water in woodlands.

Raccoons are smart and easily learn how to live in new places.

Human houses and backyards are full of things to eat and places to hide.

What Makes Raccoons Good at Living in Towns and Cities?

Raccoons can run fast to escape from danger quickly.

A running raccoon could keep up with a person on a bicycle.

Excellent climbing skills help raccoons find hiding places.

Their amazing paws help them find food. They can even turn on faucets!

Where Do Raccoons Hide?

Raccoons use up to 20 different **dens**.

They build dens in chimneys, drains, and in dark holes under woodpiles, houses, and sheds.

Raccoons are **nocturnal**, so they rest during the day and come out at night.

People may not notice they are sharing their home with a raccoon.

What Do Raccoons Eat?

Raccoons eat parts of plants, such as fruits, nuts, and grains.

They are famous for washing their food!

They hunt small animals, such as rabbits, crabs, insects, and mice.

Animal experts look at raccoon droppings to find out what they eat.

Why Do Raccoons Like Living Near People?

Raccoons can eat almost anything, and cities are full of tasty meals.

They raid trash cans, steal pet food, and dig in compost piles.

Clever raccoons work out how to get their paws on any food they spot.

They even fish in garden ponds!

What Dangers Do Raccoons Face in Towns and Cities?

City raccoons are safe from country **predators** such as coyotes.

Most city raccoons are killed by cars, before they are two or three years old.

Not everyone likes sharing a neighborhood with raccoons.

Sometimes people trap or kill raccoons to stop them from causing damage.

Do Raccoons Always Live Alone?

For most of the year, raccoons eat, rest, and sleep alone.

Males and females sometimes share **dens** in spring, when they **mate**.

The female finds the safest place she can to build a **nest**.

Two months later, up to seven **kits** are born.

How Do Baby Raccoons Learn to Live in Towns and Cities?

The mother raccoon and her **kits** do everything together.

She teaches them how to build **dens**, find food, and stay away from people.

After a year, the kits are ready to live on their own.

If they get caught raiding a trash can, they know what to do. Run!

Raccoon Spotter's Guide

Look back at the sights, sounds, and smells that tell you a raccoon might be nearby. Use these clues to go on your own city safari.

1. Raccoons have special eyes that work well in the dark. This makes their eyes shine in bright light. They may be the first things you spot!

2. Long toes make raccoon footprints look like small handprints.

3. Raccoons make lots of noise. They hiss, squeal, scream, growl, and purr. Scratching noises in a house could mean there is a raccoon inside the roof.

4. A stinky smell can be a sign that a raccoon is living inside a building.

Picture Glossary

 **den** hidden home of a wild animal

 **kit** baby raccoon

 **mate** when a male and female animal get together to have babies

 **nest** special home built by an animal, where babies are born and looked after

 **nocturnal** active mostly at night

 **predator** animal that hunts other animals for food

Find Out More

Books

Axelrod-Contrada, Joan. *Pesky Critters!: Squirrels, Raccoons, and Other Furry Invaders.* Mankato, Minn.: Capstone, 2014.

Johnson, J. Angelique. *Raccoons.* Mankato, Minn.: Capstone, 2011.

Web sites

FactHound offers a safe, fun way to find Internet sites related to this book. All of the sites on FactHound have been researched by our staff.

Here's all you do:
Visit www.facthound.com
Type in this code: 9781432988111

Index

AUG 1 5 2014